I Promised You I Wouldn't Write This

I Promised You I Wouldn't Write This

Ari Eastman

THOUGHT CATALOG BOOKS

Copyright © 2015 by The Thought & Expression Co.

All rights reserved. Published by Thought Catalog Books, a division of The Thought & Expression Co., Williamsburg, Brooklyn.

For general information and submissions: hello@thoughtcatalog.com.

First edition, 2015.

ISBN 978-1515219675

10 9 8 7 6 5 4 3 2 1

Founded in 2010, Thought Catalog is a website and imprint dedicated to your ideas and stories. We publish fiction and non-fiction from emerging and established writers across all genres.

Cover image by © iStockPhoto.com/beastfromeast

Dedication

To R: I hope you get to meet Drake one day.

To J: For being my partner-in-creepy and listening to the same poems about the same people over and over again.

To Dad: For everything. I love you.

To Martin: For giving me a second Dad.

And to Mom: For not letting me give up. Ever. You are forever my favorite thing on this planet.

Contents

Lips

He has the thinnest lips of any boy I've ever kissed.
Whenever he smiles, his top lip completely disappears
and his mole peeks out beneath always present scruff.
I wondered before he kissed me what it was going to
feel like.
Would my lips own fullness make up the difference?
Would we still find a way inside each other's mouths?
I thought a lot about his tongue.
I'm always nervous when meeting another tongue.
I have met some that forced a tango I did not ask for.
I wondered if our lips would know how to dance.
I thought about it while taking a final for my History
of Animation class.
There was something about Looney Tunes, or Disney,
but when I looked at my paper I had accidentally
written, *"He has nice teeth."*

I erased it.

But he did have nice teeth.
I liked his barely there lips and I wanted to know if they could kiss me the way I wanted to be kissed.

They did.

In his bed, half naked, the first time he kissed me, I forgot about the size. It was always about a feeling with him.

I'm still fighting that feeling.
I kissed the boy with the wide mouth, and I did not feel it.
I kissed the boy without a mole, and I did not feel it.
I kissed the boy I kissed years ago, and I did not feel it.
I do not know what it means to be kissed anymore.

Untitled

He doesn't remember our heart beats synching up perfectly.
Like a drum and a steady hand,
we formed a rhythm that was the only thing ever constant about us.

On Things That Keep Me Up At Night

I wonder what it would feel like to not speak with your heart on your tongue.
I think about mouths,
Do they feel different without this constant metallic aftertaste?
Maybe teeth are stronger when they aren't grinding against waves of anxiety.
Maybe throats aren't supposed to have a permanent lump in them.
I have spent too many nights nursing puncture wounds from my own honesty.

I am running out of bandaids, but I just keep bleeding.

These things that just keep repeating

in my life,
like why I insist on pretending I'm alright.
I'm so used to saying I'm alright,
But nobody who is awake at 3:45 in the morning
with a running monologue of the things she can't say
out loud
is
alright.
I wonder what it would feel like to not think.
Because my brain often works in overtime,
and I carry a hummingbird in my chest.
They say that most hummingbirds don't even make it
a full year.
There have been moments I wasn't sure I was going to
make it a full year,
but nobody wants to hear a suicide poem.
People want ease and nothing to cause potential
squirming.

Keep it status quo.
Don't dig too deep.
Because it's uncomfortable to hear
that I think about death more often than I think about
what I'm going to eat for dinner.
That sometimes I wish I could eat my own fears,
Swallow these insecurities I pretend I don't have.
Most hummingbirds learn to fly when they are 21 days
old
And here I am,
22 years

and still trying to figure out how I'm supposed to
survive with broken wings.
These broken things:
Like headboards,
and promises.
I wonder if he thinks about what happened the way
I'm forced to.
I wonder if drowning without water is even a thing,
Because most days, it feels like I'm struggling to
breathe.

But I am laughing.

I am always laughing.

To The Men Who Call Me Baby When I Walk Past In Shorts

I do not fit into a box.
Do not always fit snuggly in my shorts either.
My mother gave me enough heart and strength that
sometimes, I spill out on hot days.
I am more fire than I am human.
More burning building than I am woman.
I am convicted arson,
This flame of desire you think belongs to you.
Flickering amber.
My crimson footprints.
Do not mistake this ash I leave behind as
mistake.

I am the earthquake they have warned you about.
Mount Olympus gave birth to me.

I am the Goddess you are tempted to touch,
But there is a hurricane beneath my smile.
Don't you dare think you can out swim my storm.

You are not allowed to touch me.

You are not fucking allowed to touch me.

One Year

I guess it is your anniversary with her.
And now,
I am reminded it is one year,
And I am still standing.

There should be celebration for that.
But instead you will bring her flowers,
And I will look at myself in the mirror.
Force an affirmation.
Nobody says congrats
To my survival.

I cannot help counting the days
In between.
An official date now serving as a time stamp.
And how my sheets had barely even been washed.

When you became an "us"
I was still healing,
Not just metaphorically.
My body still coming to grips with what happened,
As you probably held her,
Touched her with the same hands.
Those hands,
I hated them for so long.
I do not want to believe a man like you
Could forever change
A woman like me.
But I am still uneasy when I hear sweet nothings.
Your hands become the hands
Of others,
My body suddenly not my own.
I hear honey dipped nightmares
whenever new lovers speak.

6

When I'm Waiting In The Hospital Room

It's late when she walks in.

She immediately apologizes for the temperature of her fingers,

and I tell her it's okay.

Her hand slides inside my gown and I flinch when she touches me.

"*I'm sorry*," I blurt, overcome with a strange sense of guilt.

I follow it up with a joke, like always.

Anything to ensure she doesn't think she caused me any discomfort.

I can handle frozen skin.

I am warrior.

I am product of dead father,
Sick mother,
And lost daughter.
Survival is etched into my DNA, along with every freckle,
Every curve,
Every moment I fought and fought until calluses formed,
and my body stopped working.
And I kept getting up.

I do not look like the survival story you are used to reading,
with this ear-to-ear smile I wear most of the time,
but don't mistake
I know how to write pain,
but you will not see it in my face.
I remember when I was little and had surgery for the first time I fell in love with the word stethoscope.

> The cadence.
> The rhythm.

I wanted to close my eyes when the nurse said it,

> *stethoscope.*

Like the beginning of a song and my heart would play percussion.
Fluorescent lights humming with us.

Hospitals have this strange soundtrack to them,
and you can let it haunt you or you can sing with it.

I am singing with it.

I am seeing my father in the cracks in the ceiling.
I am seeing him in these electrocardiograph lines.
I am seeing myself in the corner, watching him.
Asking God to rewind,
Begging him to poke out my eyes.
Because I do not want to watch a skeleton form before
me.
I have prayed three times in my life,
and two of them were inside a hospital.
Hospitals must know so many secrets,
the inner workings and hopes of desperate souls.
Hospitals are confessionals.
Hospitals are lonely hearts clubs.
Hospitals are start and end.
Hospitals are battle and loss
and winning
and loss again.
The nurse with the cold hands listens to my heartbeat.
"You have a very strong heart."
Yeah,
I suppose that I do.
She is the muscular organ I love to blame, even though
she has nothing to do with these decisions.
She has nothing to do with this back and forth,
my cycle of loving and running away.

Running away when someone wants to love me.
Loving those who run first.
But my feet are tired,
and they hurt.
A lot of me hurts,
but I have a strong heart.
She just keeps beating.

Drive-Ins

You wanted to love me forever.
You wrote our initials in calligraphy,
pinned futures,
like names of children.
I liked Micah.
You liked Gabriel.
We bought condoms
and bridal magazines because we were
young and embarrassed of strangers knowing
what we would do
in backseats.
Planned for upcoming years.
Maybe you would have loved me forever.
But I couldn't stay eighteen forever.
I couldn't be her
forever.

If We Had Met Another Time

If I had met you when I was 14, it would have been in the pages of my diary.
Your jawline would be page 4.
A dedicated paragraph to the amber flecks in your eyes:

Page 6.

How I was absolutely sure your hand lingered just a *teeny tiny* bit when you handed me my test in class:

Page 10.

The devastation of being so young and so sure I had fallen in love with you would be page 20.

Page 32.
Page 54.

You would be the first chapter that I rewrote and
rewrote until there was a plot line that ended with you
kissing me.

If I had met you when I was 16, we would have been
a set of illegal fireworks.
You would have been that summer night that never
ended.
We would watch the moon swap with the sun
And touch our stars.
On the surface,
hormonal teenagers
Just learning what exploration meant.
You, not my Christopher Columbus,
but someone who knew
I was always my own country.
But I was willing to share.
Maybe I wouldn't have rushed,
Sweet Sixteen.
Maybe we would have been candlelight.
And burned slowly,
steadily

If I met you at 17,
you would have asked about my Dad.
I wouldn't tell you much.
Because at 17, I pretended nothing changed.
A stranger would ask what my Dad does.

I would say, *"He's a professor."*
I do not say,
"He's a dead professor."

If I had met you at 19,
I would have already been in love with a boy with one dimple.
The only thing he held more than my hands were my anxieties,
My worries.
He held them in his chest.
He told me it was okay to give them up.
I still would have fallen in love with you, I think.
I would have seen you,
and stayed quiet.
But thought to myself,
That boy
Has a face that I have always wanted to know.
I would have swallowed a glass of guilt for dinner.
Sitting next to him.
Thinking of you.

If I had met you when I was 21,
I would not have ever wasted my time with all six foot three
of disaster waiting to unfold.
These permanent scars that still bleed.
I would not have looked at him
I would have seen through the bullshit.

Because
I would have only seen you.

I only see you.
22.
I only see you.

If I had met you when I was 23,
Maybe this time you would have seen me.

9

When You Rub His Back as He Pines for Another Girl

Please,

Get out of there.

Take off the shirt with the name of the town your Dad grew up in plastered across the front.

Put back on your dress.

Find your self control splattered next to a bottle of Makers.

Leave.

You think that if you just love him enough, he will see it.

He will understand what he is giving up and change his mind.

He will want you like he wants her.

As if it is just that simple.

Maybe he will ask how you are and mean it.
Maybe he will say something like, *"I like your smile"*
and they won't just be words to take up space.
Please,
I'm begging you to stop.
He doesn't even want you there.
Your spine is coming apart,
Vertebra losing all shape.
You skeletal girl, you.
You second choice,
You filler.
He never loved you.
Do not text back when he promises he does.
When he starts to talk about her with his body in the
crook of yours,
Leave.
Please leave for me,
Because I have forgotten how.

10

An Ode to 113

The funny thing about growing up is how often you'll find yourself going back in your mind,
Revisiting the same spots.
How you'll hunger for one more night in the treehouse.
Waking up to alarm clocks and Dad singing nonsense.
Clinging to dimming memories,
Convincing yourself things can be the same one day.
You just need to get back,
Get back to that room.
That house.
That time.
That time is moving too fast.
You didn't tell her she could move this fast.

Nobody warns you just how different something that

didn't change can feel.

The peeling paint.

The couch with tattered corners, property damage from the various canine loves of your life.

The spot on the wall that you used to anchor your nerves when anxiety took control.

Stare at it until the edges of your vision blurred.

Stare at it at 5 in the morning the night after losing your virginity,

Wondering why you couldn't feel your own heart beating.

Stare at it when the next boy told you he loved you and you were terrified,

Because you loved him too.

Stare at it years later when you've moved to a completely new city and the concept of home keeps changing.

Nobody tells you that a house can become a person.And when they decide to leave you, even if you left them first,

it can feel like the worst breakup you've ever had.

113

You were the weird kid on the block,

With a handmade chicken coop in the back that Mom was so proud of.

Faded champagne skin that never looked quite right, but something about you made me feel like I fit in,

Like I belonged.

We were both small, but flew our hearts like flags.
Anyone could see, but only a select few could raise and
lower them.

113

You saw my first kiss,
The way our knees knocked together and I pulled
away the first few times,
nervous habit kicking in.
You kept the secrets I never intended to keep.
And never told on me when I snuck an extra helping
of ice-cream.

113

I'm sorry I acted embarrassed of you sometimes.
Because you weren't the flashy palace.
You were messy and wild.
You were flawed and bruised.
I was just too insecure to realize people loved you the
same way they loved me.
Thank you for sheltering me when I was too afraid to
greet the world,
and never judging my need for solitude.
For understanding my introvert nature,
Reassuring me there was nothing wrong with being
alone.
And that it will never be the same thing as lonely.

113

I loved you so deeply.
And I will continue to love you,
Even when you no longer belong to me.
You are part of me.
I wear you in memories.
I wear you in scars.
And above all,
I wear you in my soul.

How To Fall Out Of Love

Watch it happen in the same way you first fell,
With a crushing heaviness that slowly invades your
bones
and skin,
vital organs gone haywire.
Your lungs don't function in quite the same way.
Your hands not steady guides you had spent years
trusting.
You shipwreck girl,
sailing with such ferocity,
but zero direction.

You will feel it all at once,
when lips betray ego,
Inner running monologue finally silenced with all this
heaviness,

The heaviness you cannot seem to rid.
You will burst when he grabs your hand in the grocery store,
finally say the words out loud.

"I love you."

"I am in love with you."

And for a time,
there is no heavy.
It is light, and everything you were positive it couldn't be.
There is still no direction in how you sail,
but at least his fingers can be a map.
Lighthouse bodies in the night.

The heavy will start to come back in small moments you discount.
It is nothing,
bumps and cracks,
Silence the first ping of doubt in the back of your mind.
You pull away first in embrace,
ask that he fuck you harder so you can feel.
Crack open your own ribcage,
and spill out the heavy.
The light is still there,
somewhere, you convince yourself.
So, you stay.

But it will hit you on the plane ride,
the bus,
the walk to your car,
When heart betrays brain.
Inner running monologue unable to refuse it any
longer.
The heaviness is back.
He kisses you.
You kiss back,
but you do not kiss him back.

He asks if you still love him,
and you do not kiss him back.

12

Death of Us

I hear your voice for the first time in 6 months
And you tell me I shouldn't do spoken word.

That should have been when I hung up.
That should have been the moment I said fuck you
and collapsed into a puddle in my roommate's arms.
That should have been the moment I remembered
why we fell apart in the first place.

But I kept listening.
And each and every misguided butterfly I felt when I
first answered your call got shot down,
Wing by wing.
Slingshot a grenade into the part of me that kept a door
open.
"Do something more with your talents."

Another casualty.

"Do you just run around fucking other guys now?"

Prepare the coffin.

"You never think that maybe what that guy did was your fault."

Time of death:

1:05 AM

You cannot plea intoxication to get off free.

You cannot say coping mechanism and expect me to forgive.

Your apologies hang heavy like the skeleton of the man I once thought I'd marry.

I loved you more than I knew what to do with most days.

But I do not know you now.

And this stranger you've become makes my stomach hurt.

On The Things You've Missed

I remember it so vividly,
sitting in the Orthodontist office.
A giant of a man with a Colgate smile sizing up my
own set of pearly whites.
His hands in my mouth, pointing out the crookedness.
The gap in between my two front teeth,
So small now that I know what emptiness really feels
like.
This hole in my heart just isn't as visible.

We decided I'd get Invisalign.
Mom said it would benefit my self-esteem.
You, in all sincerity, asked if it would impede my
ability to kiss.
I groaned and went bright red,
freckles dancing in contrast.

But you just wanted me to have answers to questions I might be too embarrassed to ask.

Fifteen, still waiting on the first time a boy would really see me the way I wanted to be seen.

The orthodontist chuckled,

"No, she can kiss perfectly fine with these."

And turns out, I could.

But I never got to tell you he was right.

You were privy to every detail of my schoolgirl crushes.

I trusted you the way I trusted my closest girlfriends

But you never got to interrogate any of my boyfriends.

Though,

you never really were the *let-me-get-my-shotgun* type.

You would have welcomed them with open arms.

You didn't shake hands, you hugged.

You never met a stranger, only friends you didn't really know yet.

So when the boy with brown eyes told me he loved me,

I believed it.

All I had known of love from a man was unconditional.

So when I crumbled in pieces on the kitchen floor,

watching him drive off with parts of me I could never reclaim,

I cursed your name.

I spit at whatever God or higher power or fucked up

random pattern of events took you away from me.
Nobody was going to love me that purely again

But I've started to realize that's okay.

You missed my high school graduation.
I searched for you in the stands even though I knew
better.
I cried silently in my seat, blamed it on the end of this
era.
But I didn't care to be leaving that place.
Leaving behind people I would soon forget anyway.
Those tears were solely from not seeing you.
I don't pray,
but I've started to talk to you at night.
On the things you've missed,
so that you can stay connected.
I don't want to lose you more than I already have,

I remind you of the moments I wish we could have
shared, Dad.

You didn't see me get accepted to UCLA.
You didn't see me crowned on that stage.
You never met Dylan or Nicki,
Or Ana or Alyssa,
Johanna or Sy,
Aman or Amit.
You missed my breakdowns.
My melt-downs.
My break-throughs.

My bursts of creativity.
My fuck ups.
My *what-the-fucks, I can't believe that happened.*
You never got to see me do this,
Own my words in a way I was always so afraid to do.

I wish you knew the woman I grew into.

You promised that when your light was dimming,
Mine was going to be even brighter.
You would transfer your wisdom,
Your passion,
Your zest for everything
to me,
And sometimes I forget that.
Forget I am half of you.
But now you are all of me.
Really, I've started to fall asleep during movies and eat
food way too fast. Think that maybe you really are
here,
Inside.
Somewhere.
That maybe the physical you holds my past,
but your soul lies in mine
and together,
we have my future.
That you never really died,
Dad.
In four days, when I toss my cap into the sky.
And put it on the list of just one more thing you

missed,
Maybe I'll remember that you have been here
all along.

Graduation Day

The funny thing about death is just how alive it is.
The way it sneaks up on you,
Playing Heads up 7 up.
Touches you without knowing he was coming.
Slipping into moments he should have no part in.
That every grand moment is a reminder of the loss.
The empty seat.
The empty space.
The hollow smile.
Death should not be in the ceremony.
But there he is,
Waving to me.

Wonder Woman

I grew up hearing the stories of great comic-book
heroes.
Figures large enough to overshadow boogie man fears,
How we could combat being scared of the dark
Because we had Spiderman and Superman.
The monsters in the closet could be gone in a Flash.
And we learned that Good always won over Evil.

At school, we would fight over who played which
Power Ranger,
Mutant Ninja Turtle,
Rock paper scissors for Batman, and condolences to
whoever got stuck with Robin.
These fictional characters so woven into the fabric of
my childhood that sometimes,
it was hard to remember fact from fantasy.

Wonder woman always looked so much like my mom,
with ivory skin and dark locks that hung in perfect
waves around her face.
I just assumed she was the muse for DC comics.
Maybe one of the artists happened to see her one day
on his way to work.
At 7, I didn't really calculate the math correctly on that
one.
Because Wonder Woman first appeared in 1941,
But all I could think was how much this great heroic
beauty resembled my mom.

I didn't understand how sick she was growing up.
Because she didn't miss a damn thing.
Volunteered to chaperone field trips,
Sat front and center at my kindergarden play,
Asked how school was every single day and actually
listened.
The way a mother listens to the heartbeat of her first
child,
Listens like she's never heard anything quite as
beautiful,
The way my mother made me feel with every word I
spoke.
Even when I talked,
and talked,
and talked.
Damn, I'm an only child cliche,
but I love to talk.
And she always listened.

Even when her ears were flames.
Her neck on display,
Red marks.
She burned from the inside out.
Cheeks hot,
I asked her why she looked like that at night,
Why a butterfly spread across her face?
I wished for wings that would attach to the rotten parts
of her body and fly out of her sweetness,
Choose to land far away.

I didn't realize my mother was battling her own villain.
But see,
Lupus was not just a plot line or some twist in the
story.
Lupus was not the name of a pretty girl like I first
thought when I was young.
Lupus was not Marvel,
Or DC,
Or Saturday morning cartoons.
Lupus was the reason I heard my mom cry when she
thought I was asleep because her pain was at an all time
high,
And Lupus was the reason I was never really sure if I
believed in God.
Because superheroes were supposed to beat the villain.
I had seen it enough times.
They were supposed to be invincible.
They weren't supposed to cozy up to death every
night,

Wear IVs like bracelets and hospital gowns like
couture.
But wonder woman is just a character,
And no, I'm not religious,
but if I were to use the word savior
it would be my mother–
Mother Victoria.
In the name of my father,
The sun,
And *shit*,
She is strength and wisdom,
And an incredible badass.
This muse who wakes every day
and chooses to be a light.
Sunshine when others would be thunderstorms.
I have learned that no, in fact, my mother is not
wonder woman
Because my mother is so,
So
much more.

16

Waking Up

You are the only thing I crave more than coffee in the morning.
I don't know which addiction is easier to break.
I like you both too much to find out.

17

On Dating Artists

My poet friends and I always joke about the danger in dating people like us:

The ones who will turn empty promises into love songs.

The ones who will get on a stage and share things they can't find the courage to tell you without an audience.

The ones who swallow antidepressants in the form of words.

And let me tell you,

We are not easy people to impress either.

When we are constantly surrounded with metaphors

about flowers and the moon, even the most sincere compliments seem stolen from Nicholas Sparks novels.

We will read your confessions like a romcom script.

We will spell check your love notes.

Don't ever think you can fool us.

We choose when we want to be fooled.

You did not outsmart us, you just became our next great tragedy.

Do not fall for a writer.

We break our own hearts already.

Broken

My bed still has the crack we made.
It's almost funny.
My heart has the same one.

Home

I thought I would build a nest in you.

Collect all the branches and twigs in the backyard.

Glue the mess.

Lace fingertips.

Construct a home for just us two.

But,

I've never been good at making things out of nothing.

So when the pieces collapsed,

Our bones splintered,

And you walked away,

Maybe I always knew.

20

Frog

Last night, you reached for all of me and I swung my wholeness to the other side of the bed.

I did not do so intentionally.

I have just never known how to settle at night when others turn statue.

I am not stillness.

I am anxiety and nerves, and nothing that can be lullabied into a quiet peace.

I am the coffee spill on your lap.

I am the shitty parking job.

I am mess and it's true that even you do not bring me to peace,

But you have become my piece.

You scooped me into your cocoon, clung tight to the reassurance of body next to body.

I wondered if you even knew it was me you were holding.

I thought maybe it was just impulse.

Physical reaction.

But your hands searched for mine at each clock strike,

and I met them every time.

I still try to meet them knowing full well when the sun rises,

I won't be able to remember the way your index finger traced the indents of my knuckles.

Love, you are not mine to call Love, but you keep singing to me in these daydreams.

Love, I wish for the saline to dry from your cheeks.

Love, I want to hire a meteorologist or therapist or goddamn magician to free the darkness from your grey matter.

I guess I just want to find the light for you.

When you rain, I am drenched in this melodramatic heartache.

It sounds simple to say,

but I never want to see you hurt.

I would pick apart my own heart strings and use them to tie yours back together.

I am okay bleeding out, so long as you are given a new chance, a new life.

Love,

This is how I know you are worthy of that name, Love.

That what I feel for you is selfless, irrational

Unconditional.

And something I have tried to understand, but love is not an easy concept to pluck from a Dictionary,

Or Thesaurus

Or Google search.

Maybe my soul knew you were that word,

Love,

because drunk, in the middle of Hollywood, you approached me,

Awkward and weird.

And still, I gave you my number and uncaged a thousand butterflies from my throat.

In your almost neon turquoise sweatshirt,

I can't believe I was the sober one

Now knowing how intoxicated I am with every sip I'm given of you.

Love, I know that addiction is not a good word.

But I don't know what else to call this need to fill you with everything you don't yet have.

I know that you will never be mine.

When you are so lost and broken and crumble from memories that sting you while I sit waiting with bandaids,

and a first aid kit of promises that one day, you'll be okay.

One day you will not need me.

Right now, Love, you need me.

And I need you.

This is messy,

and not the romance I first thought when you kissed me.

Mouth full of maybes,

your mouth is now full of, *"Baby, this is only to help me get through the night."*

and Love,

I am doing the same thing.

We are doing the same thing.

I Promised You I Wouldn't Write This

In bed, you held me and asked, "You're going to write about this, aren't you?"

And when one gets tangled in the sheets and metaphors of a poet, it's a fair question.

You know what I have written before.

The way I weave together our memories like an unfinished obituary.

How I leave traces of last times, first times, one more times throughout word documents.

Dusty notebooks.

Post-its to remind myself why I keep coming back to write one more chapter.

You have every reason to believe I would write that night into another elegy.

But I told you I wouldn't.
I promised you I wouldn't.
And this,
This is not about last night.
Because there are some moments that even the softest
tongue can never do justice.
Moments I never dare to expose for the sake of art,
for the sake of healing,
For the sake of feeling like I'm doing something with
all this heavy.
This is not my escapism.
This is my honesty.
You are the shot of whisky that turns my throat from
a body part to a cathedral.
I am broken sparrow who flies back to your window
because I heard you like my singing.
You are land mines of potential.
I am not afraid of the explosion.
You think I will write about that night,
But all I can think of is your stardust eyes.
I run out of words when they stare back into mine.
You speak in tailspin.
But our fingers have always known when to be quiet.

You, a lone wolf.
I, the full moon.
I choose to shine when you need your path
illuminated.
I don't always glow bright enough.
You don't always howl loud enough.

But we were meant to find ourselves in this mess,
this heart break and heart broken.
Maybe we are both bleeding for a purpose.
Make handmade tourniquet out of our laughter.
It can be so easy sometimes.
When you stop thinking,
And I stop dreaming.
And we sit and laugh,
Let our fingers do the speaking.
I will not write of that night.
But I will tell the story of you.
The same way the bullfrogs coo under an August sky,
slowly and deeply,
And when the rest of the world goes to sleep.

22

Oceans

There should be a sign in this water that says,
"No fishing allowed."
The supply is running low,
insatiable hunger for these scales will end in extinction.
Salmon swimming backwards,

I bend my spine in ways it was never supposed to go
for you.
It will all run dry soon enough.
A bearded stranger cast his line towards me, but
instead,
I just bleed dry for you.
Swallow ink and continue penning verses for you.
Catch and release,
Find my way back again.
Swimming backwards.

I am too hooked on tomorrows that will never happen
with the one
who never intended for me to swim into his net.
Stockholm syndrome,
in love with the diver who plucked me from Atlantis,

Caught
and released.

Now,
it feels so much colder.
I never realized the ocean was this dark before.

23

R

I love you in the moments we don't say what we feel.
When we are drunk on laughter,
And sometimes,
actual drinks.
The night you kissed me, but don't remember.
And it kept me awake for weeks.
Grabbed me, half asleep, pulled me straight into your lips.
Kissed me.
Held me.
Touched me.
You do not remember this.
I do.
I love you in the moments you are pissing me off.
When you are pushing my buttons,
testing the limits of what I will say is funny.

What I will say is crossing a line.
I cross all the lines,
Boundaries,
Counties,
Cities,
Rationality,
Hook line and sink.
This red string theory.
We are unbreakable.
I am forever here, waiting for when you need me.
I love you in the outrageousness
of continuing to love you
when I know you do not love me back
in the way I think you should.
You might.
You will.
You won't.
I don't know,
I am not clair voyant.
Though I wish I could know why
the universe will not allow me to let you go.

I love you in commercials.
Men that look like you.
I love you in comments to my mother.
I love you in literature.
Books.
Quotes.
Songs that set my throat on fire,
Singing,

I love you in words
and words
and words.
I love you in nonsense.
I love you in your fears
Doubts,
And insecurities.
I love you in your desire to let me in,
even when it isn't your first choice.
You let me in,
in ways you don't always.
You let me in,
when building fences would have been easier.
You have hugged me.
And kissed.
And laughed.
And fucked.
And hurt.
And hugged again.

I love you in your mole.
I love you in your defense mechanisms.
I love you shirtless in your bed, with the corner sheet
coming off.
I love you under neon lights with self-serve Frozen
Yogurt stations.

I love you for this,
and so much more.
I can never explain,

but you are the last face I see before I sleep
and the name I check for on my phone when I wake.

24

On Knowing What You Want

My mother used to tell me that even as a young child,
I was in love with concept of love.

I would gather up my various stuffed animals and line
them up on the couch.

One by one, I'd ask each bachelor and bachelorette
what they were seeking in a partner.

And I, the matchmaker, would see what I could do for
them.

Nip, the orange cat with one eye, was seeking a tender
feline to understand his occasional moodiness.

George, an oversized Simba (who always felt more
like a George to me) yearned for someone to go on
adventures with,

Someone to lick his wounds clean when he got a little
too wild.

Someone to jump over fences with.
Chase gazelle.
Basically just do some crazy lion shit together.

Nicey, the plastic lobster, who was probably the weirdest toy I had (but I loved him just a little more than the others) wanted someone to look past his giant claws and realize he was just a sweet, docile crustacean. His name was Nicey, for crying out loud.

And I vowed, no matter how long it took, I would pair up each and every one of them.
I would not rest until romance bloomed for every tiger, bear, Barbie, and dragon in my house.
I picked up my bow, and equipped with an overwhelming amount of optimism,
I shot an arrow into the hearts of them all,
All of them, except for one.
Floppy.
A delicate mouse with ears twice as big as his face.
He couldn't ever tell me what it was he was looking for,
so eventually, I stopped asking.
And it took 18 years to realize why I never pushed him.
18 years to realize why he was the only one I couldn't find a perfect match for.
18 years to finally understand that I'm Floppy,
with my ears a little too big, and indecisiveness about almost everything.

I'm not sure I've ever really known what I want.
That I will speak so highly of romance, but run away
when it gets too real.
I boast of big plans and goals,
but let opportunities slip through my fingers without
even trying to grasp them.

Floppy and I are just trying to find that thing.
The one.
The place.
The something that tells us,
Yes,
This is where you belong.
This is what you have been looking for all along.
Maybe we aren't supposed to know what it is yet.
Maybe we never really do.
We place such pressure on ourselves to have it all
figured out,
When there should be no shame in being honest.
In being Floppy and saying, "I have no fucking clue
what I'm looking for."
You're looking.
Give yourself some credit for that.
To my lost ones:
My graduates,
My dreamers,
My pessimists,
My hopefuls,
My lovers,
My broken hearted someones,

My ones just barely hanging on,
You don't always need to know what you're doing.
Just keep doing.
Keep being.
You are not alone, so please stay.
Please.
Stay with me.

Dear Body

I love you,
madly, deeply.
Truly.
For everything you are and everything you aren't.
From the slight curve of your spine,
to your child-like hands.
The scars on your back from picking.
Trying to pick your flaws away.
Small when you should be big.
Big when you should be small.
I love every piece of you.
You are beautiful,
And I am so sorry I don't tell you that enough.

On Lessons I Keep Learning

If you have to convince someone to be with you,
If you have to sell yourself like a used car,
Pitch your good attributes, boasting all the good miles
you have left.
The miles you could use to take them anywhere they
need,
Promise them glamorous adventure and safety.
That you would never break down and leave them
stranded.
Though your engine often sputters, let's face it, you've
never known how to be smooth.
You imagine he'd tell you your words taste like honey,
when really you're just an oil spill.
And if he flicks his cigarette towards you,
and doesn't even look back to see if you're burning,

You should walk away.
You need to walk away.

Because you're not a damn car.
And if your value is not understood right away, don't waste your time.
Don't waste your tears.
You'll only drown in your own self-doubt, but nobody will be there to save you.
You will just keep burning.

When I Drunk Text You

There was that night I went to bed at 10:30 pm with an alarm set on my phone for only a few hours later.

2:15 am, Prince plays.
Because for some reason, I thought "Kiss" was a good song to use as my alarm clock.
And now, I flinch when I hear his high pitched groan.

2:15 am, Prince sings to me.

I will text you at 2:15 am so you think I am drunk.
So I can blame this inability to let go on a bottle of Jack.
Or Captain.
or Hennessy.

Anything.

2:17 you have texted me first.

I wonder if you set an alarm too.
I leave an extra letter to support my alibi of alcohol.
"i miss youu"

I miss you.

You say, *"Remember that time I asked to hear your poetry?"*
I say, *"Which time?"*
"You did it to my wall because you said looking at me made you nervous."

It's true.
Reciting poetry to the muse would make the bravest writer sweat.

"I liked when you did that. I like hearing your poems."

My throat is closing.
There are too many words that want to escape, but it's only my fingers that are speaking anyways.

You are out at a bar.
You make a joke about a girl.
I want to throw up and I have not been drinking.

You ask, *"Have you found what you're looking for? Are you ready to come back home?"*
I don't respond quickly enough.

"You should come back."

I throw my phone across the room.
And then apologize to no one.

2:45 you say, *"Go to bed. You're drunk."*

I tell you I'm not really that drunk.
But you are the worst hangover I've ever had.

I Have Decided I Do Not Love You Anymore

I do not reread your text messages.

I do not buy you small knick knacks at the flea market with the $10 I had originally planned to spend on myself.

I do not think about you when I wake up.

I do not choke on my own anxiety when you do not respond.

I do not think about you when I go to sleep.

I do not love you anymore.

I love you.

I do not love you anymore.

Ashes

I am a volcano

that has never known how to be still.

But when the smoke settles,
I will still be here.

Don't you see?
I'm still here.

Living Again

I guess this is what some would call getting better.
This is healing,
Crawling back into my skin,
then peeling back the scabs,
bit by bit.
Exposing flesh.
Dripping droplets of lost girl,
of 20 something girl,
of choking on exhaust girl,
and admitting it's okay
to start all over again.

This is not swallowing cyanide pills in the form of self
doubt and sabotage.
I stopped looking for a way
to carve his name into my DNA.

Thinking logic and reasoning were in my favor.
There *has* to be reason.
This is stopped looking for a reason.
This is breaking the addiction
to oncoming headlights,
and lonely.
Darkness and manic.
Waiting in bars
for people who don't come
for you,
lost girl,
I started getting better.

I started living again.
I'm living again.

About The Author

Ari Eastman is a spoken word poet, writer, and YouTuber who will tell you random facts about sharks, if you're into that kind of thing. Plus, her mom thinks she's really funny. You can ask her.